ARISTOTLE

Brian Williams

Heinemann Library
Chicago, Illinois

© 2002 Reed Educational & Professional Publishing
Published by Heinemann Library,
an imprint of Reed Educational & Professional Publishing,
Chicago, Illinois

Customer Service 888-454-2279

Visit our website at www.heinemannlibrary.com

Designed by Celia Floyd
Illustrated by Jeff Edwards and Joanna Brooker
Originated by Ambassador Litho Ltd
Printed by Wing King Tong in Hong Kong

06 05 04 03 02
10 9 8 7 6 5 4 3 2 1

Library of Congress Cataloging-in-Publication Data
Williams, Brian, 1959-
  Aristotle / Brian Williams.
      p. cm. -- (Historical biographies)
Includes bibliographical references (p.   ) and index.
Summary: Presents an account of Aristotle's life, from birth to death,
and explores his impact on history and the world.
  ISBN 1-58810-563-6 (HC), 1-58810-997-6 (Pbk.)
 1. Aristotle--Juvenile literature. 2.
Scientists--Greece--Biography--Juvenile literature. 3.
Philosophers--Greece--Biography--Juvenile literature. [1. Aristotle. 2.
Scientists. 3. Philosophers.] I. Title. II. Series.
  B481 .W55 2002
  185--dc21

2001003658

Acknowledgments
The author and publishers are grateful to the following for permission to reproduce copyright material:
Cover photograph: The Art Archive
pp. 4, 7, 8, 11, 12, 13, 17, 20, 23, 24, 26, 29 The Art Archive; pp. 6, 10, 18, 25, 28 Ancient Art and Architecture; pp. 9, 22 British Museum; p. 14 AKG; p. 15 Corbis; pp. 16, 19 Scala; p. 21 University of Manchester; p. 27 The Travel Library.

Special thanks to Rebecca Vickers for her comments during the preparation of this book.

Some words are shown in bold, **like this.** You can find out what they mean by looking in the glossary.

Many Greek names and terms may be found in the pronunciation guide.

Contents

A Land of Gods and Thinkers

Aristotle of Greece was one of the greatest thinkers who ever lived. Although he was born more than 2,300 years ago, his ideas are still talked about today. Aristotle and his ideas helped shape Western **civilization.**

Aristotle was one of the most important **philosophers** of ancient Greece. Greek philosophers asked questions such as "What is true?" and "What is the best form of **government?**" Aristotle was one of the first scientists to study animals and plants closely, but he was just as interested in art, religion, how countries are governed, and the way we think. He was a teacher, too. His most famous student was Alexander the Great, one of the greatest **conquerors** in history.

Aristotle's Greece

Aristotle's Greece was the birthplace of **democracy**—the form of "government by the people" used in many countries today. Ancient Greece was a collection of small city-states. Each city-state had its own government and ruled the villages, farms, and ports in the surrounding area. The Greeks had many gods. Every town had temples and statues to these gods who, people believed, looked down on Greece from Mount Olympus.

◄ Greek sculptors made **busts** and statues of famous people. This is a bust of Aristotle.

Because Greece had little good farmland, many people left to settle in **colonies** elsewhere. In this way, Greek ideas spread to North Africa, Italy, and Spain.

Aristotle spent many years in Athens, a city famous for its **politicians,** writers, and teachers. He wrote in Greek, but his writings were later copied into other languages and studied by people in many countries. For hundreds of years, people thought Aristotle was right about practically everything. Modern science has shown that, as a scientist, Aristotle was sometimes wrong. Yet he left so many important ideas that people still want to read what he had to say.

▲ Greece is a peninsula—a piece of land sticking out into the sea—that is surrounded by many islands. Aristotle was born in northern Greece, at Stagira, but spent much of his time in Athens, Asia Minor, and the island of Lesbos. He died at Chalcis.

Key dates

384 B.C.E.	Aristotle is born
367 B.C.E.	Aristotle travels to Athens to study with Plato
344 B.C.E.	Aristotle studies nature on the island of Lesbos
336 B.C.E.	Alexander becomes king of Greece
335 B.C.E.	Aristotle opens the Lyceum in Athens
322 B.C.E.	Aristotle dies

Watch the dates

"B.C.E." after a year date means before the common era. This is used instead of the older abbreviation "B.C." The years are counted backwards toward zero. After this, the years go forward, starting with 1 C.E. (common era).

A Doctor's Son

Aristotle was born in 384 B.C.E., in the small town of Stagira, on the northwest shore of the Aegean Sea. Aristotle's mother came from Chalcis, on the island of Euboea. His father, Nicomachus, was a doctor and **court physician** to King Amyntas II of Macedonia, a kingdom in the north of Greece.

Welcoming a son

Nicomachus, like many fathers, would have been pleased to have a son. Seven days after Aristotle's birth, there would have been a party. Garlands of olive leaves decorated the house, friends brought presents, and Nicomachus went to the temple to thank the gods for his new son.

Aristotle's hometown

Like most Greek towns, Stagira had an open square, called the *agora,* used for markets and public meetings. Around this square were small houses with sloping roofs of reddish clay tiles, as well as elegant wood and stone temples. Nicomachus must have been a leading **citizen** in this small community.

▶ This picture from a wall carving in Greece shows Asclepius, the god of healing, treating a man with an injured arm.

▲ Every Greek town had at least one temple, where people left gifts for the gods. These are the ruins of the temple of the goddess Athena in the city of Delphi.

Medicine in Greece

Doctors in Greece practiced a mixture of medicine and magic. The god of healing was Asclepius. People prayed to him when they or their relatives were ill. Nicomachus probably gave his patients medicines made from herbs, and performed surgical operations—without painkilling drugs. He probably also knew of some new ideas put forward by a doctor named Hippocrates, who believed in practical cures based on knowing how the body worked.

Sons and daughters

Greek fathers welcomed a boy baby. A son would grow up to be a citizen, inherit the family property, and support his aging parents. A daughter could not do these things, because in Greece, women did not have the same freedoms and rights as men.

Aristotle's Childhood

Nicomachus was rich, so Aristotle's mother had **slaves** as servants and a nurse to help look after her young son. Poor women had to go out often, to fetch **charcoal** for the cooking fire or water from the well, but the doctor's wife probably stayed at home most of the time. A rich woman ran her household, told the servants what to do, and made sure the family had enough clothes. Much of her time was spent spinning and weaving. She went out only to visit the temple, the hairdresser, or perhaps a woman friend. When she did travel, a slave usually went with her. Her husband ordered the groceries from the market, and the goods were delivered to the house. When Nicomachus attended a feast at the king's palace, his wife probably stayed at home. Respectable women did not go to parties.

Meeting a prince

When Aristotle was three, his parents would have celebrated his birthday with prayers and a special meal. Little boys were given a present—a small decorated pottery jug, like those men owned. By the time he was five, Aristotle probably had a **tutor.** This would have been an educated slave who taught the boy the letters of the Greek alphabet.

▶ **The Greek alphabet had 27 letters, some of which look like the letters in the alphabet we use today.**

As Aristotle grew older, his father must have taken him to the king's court. King Amyntas had three sons, and the youngest, Philip, was just two years younger than Aristotle. He was probably already training to be a soldier.

Athens and Sparta

Athens was the richest and most artistic of all the Greek cities; Sparta was the most warlike. The Spartans trained their boys for war. The Athenians had the best navy in Greece, but their leaders were as famous for making speeches as for fighting. Athenian **citizens governed** themselves. The Spartans, who disliked new ideas such as **democracy**, were ruled by a small group of warrior-nobles. Spartan women could own their houses while women in Athens could not.

▶ Greek children had many toys that are still familiar playthings today. This Greek doll has arms and legs that can move.

Children's toys

Children in Greece spent a lot of their time playing outdoors. They flew kites, played board games with dice, and had wooden and pottery dolls with painted faces and jointed arms and legs. Babies had pottery potty-chairs and feeding cups, in the same shapes as modern plastic ones.

Family Life

Aristotle left no account of his childhood. We can figure out roughly what his early life would have been like from what **historians** and **archaeologists** have discovered about ancient Greek family life.

A Greek house

Aristotle's home would have been a typical house of the time, made of stone, mud brick, and timber, with a clay tile roof. An ancient Greek house had few windows on the outside walls, but did have an inner courtyard. Men and women had separate rooms in the house. Aristotle would have slept on a bed with ropes strung across a wooden frame. His few clothes and toys were probably stored in baskets or wooden chests.

Aristotle the animal lover

Many Greek children kept pets—cats, dogs, birds, tortoises, and even snakes and lizards. Aristotle almost certainly had pets, for he loved nature.

▶ The scene on this Greek vase shows the olive harvest. Men with long sticks are hitting the tree branches to make the olives fall to the ground.

◀ A Greek woman wore a long linen dress, called a *chiton,* and put on a *himation,* partly covering her head, when she went out.

Clothes

As a child, Aristotle would have worn a short **tunic** and run around barefoot. Young men wore short kilts or tunics made from wool or linen. Older men wore ankle-length tunics, sometimes with a cloak called a *himation* on top. **Slaves** and workers often wore just a **loincloth.**

Many Greeks were farmers. They grew barley and wheat for bread-making, and grapes for making wine. They also grew olives, to be eaten and also to be crushed for their oil. The oil was used in cooking and burned in clay lamps at night. There were fishermen, too.

Meal times

For breakfast, Aristotle would have eaten bread soaked in wine or milk. Lunch would have been bread and cheese, with olives, grapes, or figs. For their evening meal, people ate barley porridge, with beans, lettuce, cabbage, carrots, and onions, and sometimes fish. Most Greeks ate meat only on special feast days.

School Days

Aristotle probably received his first lessons in science and medicine from his father. Around the age of seven, Aristotle would have started school. In Greece, only boys from wealthy families went to school. Girls were taught at home by their mothers.

Greek schools

Most Greek schools had fewer than twenty students. The boys wrote on wooden tablets coated with wax, using a pointed stick called a stylus as a pen. They did math using an abacus, moving beads on wire on a wooden frame. Aristotle would have studied history and learned parts of Homer's long poems by heart. He also knew the speeches of Pericles, a famous Athenian leader (490–429 B.C.E.).

At fourteen, Aristotle would have played sports well. He and his friends would practice on an open, sandy field. They wrestled, ran races, and threw the **javelin** and **discus**. The best athletes might take part in the **Olympic Games**, held every four years to honor Zeus, king of the gods.

▶ This statue shows an athlete throwing the discus. Greek athletes did not wear clothes in races and other competitions.

The theater and friends

Most Greeks loved the theater, and Aristotle would almost certainly have gone. Theaters were hollowed out of hillsides. The audience sat on stone benches arranged in rings down the hill. The stage was at the bottom. Masked actors performed comedies or sad, serious tragedies.

As he grew older, Aristotle would have shared the company of grown men who came to his house for dinner. Men did not eat with women. They lay on couches, talking while they drank wine and ate with their fingers from dishes carried in by **slaves**.

▶ Greek actors wore masks. The expression on the mask showed the character's age and feelings. The large mouth helped to make the actor's voice louder.

Slaves and freemen

One in four people in Greece was a slave. Slaves were usually prisoners captured in war. They were sold or hired for work in the town market. Most slaves were treated kindly. Slaves could be freed, and a few eventually became wealthy businessmen.

The Quest for Knowledge

In 367 B.C.E., when he was seventeen, Aristotle traveled south to Athens to go to the **university** there. The school was called the Academy. It was run by Greece's most famous teacher, Plato.

Life in Athens

Athens was the biggest and most beautiful city in Greece. Over the city stood the Acropolis—a hill with the gleaming temple of the Parthenon on the top. About 250,000 people lived in the city. It must have seemed to Aristotle that they spent most of their time talking about **politics.** Pericles, a famous ruler of Athens, once said that someone with no interest in politics had no business living in Athens!

A democratic city

Athens was not ruled by a king. It was a **democracy,** with the laws made by an assembly of freemen called **citizens.** The citizens could vote to get rid of any **politician** who annoyed them. That person was then sent into **exile.**

◄ This picture shows pieces of broken pottery, called *ostraka.* Athenian citizens could vote for a politician they wanted to exile by writing his name on *ostraka.*

A brilliant student

Plato soon saw that Aristotle was his most brilliant student. The two must have argued for hours. Plato said that a picture of a table was not as good as a real table; Aristotle wanted to know how the table was made. Plato wanted to know about a person's **soul**, but Aristotle was just as interested in what went on inside a person's stomach!

Plato no doubt offered his young friend good advice. He would have warned him that clever people often made powerful enemies. Plato's own teacher, Socrates, had been accused of dishonoring the gods. He was condemned to death.

▲ This 1510 painting by the Italian artist Raphael shows Plato (left) and Aristotle (right) walking and talking together.

Plato

Plato's real name was Aristocles. "Plato" was a nickname that meant "broad-shouldered." Plato had left Athens in disgust after Socrates (469–399 B.C.E.) was sentenced to death. He returned to Athens in 387 B.C.E. and started the Academy in a grove of trees. The Academy was like a very early university. Plato was 60 when Aristotle came to study with him.

A School of His Own

For twenty years, Aristotle studied and worked in Plato's school, and the two men became close friends. Plato was very interested in ideas and in questions of right and wrong. Aristotle was more practical—he wanted to learn about the natural world and how it worked.

The student traveler

When he was not in school, it is likely that Aristotle traveled around Greece, usually on foot. As he wandered, he studied plants and animals, listened to people's stories, and observed the stars and changing seasons.

Leaving the Academy

Around 347 B.C.E., Plato died at the age of 81. Aristotle wrote that Plato had shown "by his own life, how to be happy is to be good." The Academy was to be run by Plato's nephew, Speusippus. Aristotle, now 37, decided it was time to start a school of his own.

◄ This Roman mosaic shows a scene at Plato's Academy.

Aristotle sailed across the Aegean Sea to Asia Minor (modern Turkey), where two old friends were living in a town called Assus. The local ruler, Hermeias of Atarneus, was a soldier who had made a fortune from gold mines. With money to spend on learning, he invited Aristotle to lead a new school in Assus.

Hermeias became a student, a friend, and before long, his father-in-law—because Aristotle married Hermeias's adopted daughter, Pythias. The newlyweds soon had a daughter, whom they named Pythias, too.

▼ After Aristotle's wedding, there would have been a party. These servants are bringing in the food and drink for a feast.

Marriage in the Greek world

In Greece, girls married at fourteen or fifteen, but men often married late, like Aristotle. Perhaps he remembered Plato's warning that it was a crime for a man not to marry! Like most Greek men, Aristotle lived apart from his wife much of the time.

The Island of Lesbos

After his first wife died, we know that Aristotle married again. His new wife was named Herpyllis, and the couple had a son, named Nicomachus.

Three years after his arrival at Assus, Aristotle decided to spend some time on the island of Lesbos. He made the short voyage to the island in one of the many small ships that sailed the Aegean Sea.

Naturalist on the island

Lesbos had once been the home of Greece's best woman poet, Sappho. Aristotle enjoyed poetry and was developing his own ideas about how it should be written, but his main interest now was **biology**. For two summers, he wandered the island as a **naturalist**.

Studying sea creatures

On Lesbos, Aristotle did what scientists today call "fieldwork." He watched birds and insects, and wandered along the beaches, picking up shells and peering into pools for sea creatures. He made notes of everything he saw.

▶ This wall painting from the island of Thera (modern-day Santorini) shows a fisherman with his catch.

Aristotle thought that if scientists were to make sense of the natural world, they must look at everything in detail. Scientists must believe what they saw, not what people told them. He also wondered about life and death, and about the **soul.** Was it separate from the body, as Plato thought, or were body and soul linked in some mysterious way?

▲ Greek trading ships had one sail. Warships like this had a single sail as well, but were also rowed by men with long oars.

The Greeks at sea

Aristotle would have learned much about life at sea during his Aegean travels. The Greeks sailed in wooden ships, each with a single mast and a square sail. Like other sea travelers, Aristotle probably wore his valuables in a bag around his neck, so that anyone finding his drowned body could pay for its burial.

A Royal Summons

Aristotle was dragged away from this pleasant life of research in 342 B.C.E., when Hermeias received a message from Philip of Macedonia.

Philip's plans

Philip had become king of Macedonia in 359 B.C.E., after the deaths of his older brothers, Alexander and Perdiccas. He was planning to rule all of Greece, and wanted Hermeias to join him in fighting against **Persia.** By going to war, Philip hoped to unite all the Greeks under his leadership.

Philip also had a personal request. He and his queen, Olympias, had a teenage son, Alexander, who needed a **tutor.** Hermeias had recommended the cleverest teacher in Assus—Aristotle.

Philip invited Aristotle to come to his court in Pella and teach his son. It was a summons that Aristotle could hardly refuse.

◀ **This painted dish shows a Greek soldier called a hoplite. Hoplites wore armor made of metal and leather, and helmets, and carried spears and round shields.**

The journey to Pella

So Aristotle packed his notes and the baskets full of shells, dried starfish, and pressed flowers that he had collected. He crossed the Aegean Sea once more, with his family and servants. They finished their journey on foot. Pella must have seemed a small, rough city to someone who had spent so long in Athens, but Aristotle received a warm welcome.

Prince Alexander was thirteen when Aristotle met him. Philip wanted his son to have the best education—quickly. War was coming, and Alexander would have to ride into battle alongside his father.

▶ Scientists at Manchester University in England made this model of King Philip's head, based on a skull found in his tomb. It shows the scar of an arrow wound.

Aristotle the teacher

Aristotle believed that education should "mold" a child into a good **citizen**. Children should first be taught to be fit and athletic. Then they should study reading and writing, music, gymnastics, drawing, and mathematics. Older students should study literature and geography, before going on to explore every kind of knowledge.

Teaching the Great

For the next three years, the teenage prince and the middle-aged scientist worked together. Aristotle found Alexander an eager student, interested in **philosophy**, medicine, and history.

Aristotle and Alexander

Eventually, the **tutor's** work ended. Philip left his son in charge of Macedonia while he was away fighting, and Alexander became a soldier. After Philip's victory over Athens at the Battle of Chaeronea in 338 B.C.E., Macedonia controlled all of Greece.

In Athens, people feared their new ruler would end their freedom. Philip did not speak Greek well, so to the Athenians he was seen as something of a **barbarian.** The king, however, respected Aristotle's wisdom. Aristotle probably helped to write the **treaty** with Athens, urging all Greeks to fight **Persia**, after the terrible news came that his friend Hermeias had been captured by the Persians and put to death.

▲ Homer's poem the *Iliad* tells the story of the Trojan War. This vase painting shows one of the heroes of the story, Achilles, killing the Amazon queen Penthesilea.

Advice to a future conqueror

Hermeias had died bravely, and Aristotle wrote a poem in his memory, comparing Hermeias to the hero Achilles. It is possible that he told Alexander to avenge his friend's death by overthrowing the king of Persia.

It is hard to tell how much Alexander followed what Aristotle taught him. Though Aristotle believed Greek city-states should be free, Alexander ruled as the all-powerful leader of an **empire**. Aristotle thought Greek ways were better than those of barbarians, but Alexander came to admire and copy many Eastern customs.

▶ This marble **bust** is of Aristotle's most famous student, Alexander the Great.

How Greeks fought

Most Greek soldiers fought on foot, marching in a tight mass called a phalanx. A soldier's weapons included a long spear, a **javelin** or throwing spear, a **bronze** sword, and a bow. Many members of the Macedonian army were particularly strong horsemen.

War and Peace

Aristotle and his family returned to his hometown of Stagira around 339 B.C.E. He was probably glad to be away from Pella, where there was trouble at the royal court.

Philip's death

In 337 B.C.E., King Philip divorced Queen Olympias and married a new wife. This led to a furious quarrel between the king and Alexander. Then, in 336 B.C.E. Philip was murdered—supposedly by a young noble. Although some people accused Alexander of plotting his father's death. Aristotle did not think so. In his book *Politics,* he described Philip's death as an example of how a ruler might be removed by one man, acting on a personal grudge.

▲ This piece of a Roman mosaic shows Alexander (far left, on horseback) leading his army to victory over the Persian king, Darius III, at the Battle of Issus.

▲ Athens was the home of Greek **democracy**. Aristotle enjoyed teaching in the city, but like many important men, he had enemies there, too.

Alexander goes to war

In 335 B.C.E., Aristotle returned to Athens. He was nearly 50 years old. The new king, Alexander, crushed a **revolt** in Thebes, but spared Athens. He visited the **oracle** at Delphi, where he was told that he would never be defeated. In 334 B.C.E., Alexander marched east with over 35,000 soldiers to conquer Asia.

Back in Athens

In Athens, Aristotle was friendly with a Macedonian general, Antipater, who was left in charge while Alexander was away. Among the men Alexander had taken with him to Asia was Callisthenes, Aristotle's nephew. In 328 B.C.E., Alexander accused Callisthenes of **treason** and had him killed. This action angered Aristotle.

Home in the city

City life suited Aristotle. He enjoyed browsing in Athens' book market, where **papyrus scrolls** of plays, speeches, and poetry were sold. The city was full of life and ideas. Plato had written about an ideal city, but Aristotle thought that real cities showed human **civilization** at its best.

The Lyceum

The last thirteen years of Aristotle's life (335–322 B.C.E.) were spent setting up his own school in Athens, called the Lyceum. Its students met in a grove of trees just outside the city. Most of the writings by Aristotle that have survived are notes of the lectures that he gave to his students, while walking beneath the trees. The teachers and students ate together, argued about many topics, and read **scrolls** in a library that had been paid for by Alexander.

A great man

Aristotle was now a great man in a city of great men. **Busts** and statues of him show someone who looks ready to talk **politics**, discuss poetry, or explain why crabs have shells. He was wealthy and dressed nicely. He liked fine cloaks and rings.

◄ Aristotle and his students spent much of their time walking and discussing, like the **philosophers** on this Greek vase.

Aristotle's death

Alexander had conquered an **empire** stretching as far as India, but in 323 B.C.E., he died suddenly in Babylon. The Greek world was thrown into turmoil. General Antipater was called away from Athens. Aristotle, "the Macedonians' friend," became a target for hate. Aristotle feared he would be killed.

Aristotle and his wife fled to Chalcis, on the island of Euboea. He made his will—leaving instructions that his **slaves** be freed after his death and that statues of the god Zeus and the goddess Athena be erected in his hometown of Stagira. He began to complain of stomach pains, and in 322 B.C.E. he died, at the age of 62.

▲ The island of Euboea (also known as Evvoia), just off the east coast of Greece, may have been Aristotle's burial place.

Aristotle's grave?

Aristotle's mother was born on the island of Euboea. In 1896, **archaeologists** working there found a **tomb** containing a skull, seven gold diadems (headbands), two styluses, a pen, and a small clay statue of a man. It is possible that the tomb may have been Aristotle's, or may have some link with his family.

What Aristotle Left to the World

Aristotle passed on much of what Greeks before him had thought, and added many more of his own ideas. Only parts of his last great work, *On Philosophy,* remain, but it has probably affected Western thought more than any other book of **philosophy.** The titles of other books by Aristotle show how wide his interests were: *Physics,* about why things change; *On the Soul,* about the **soul** and the body; *Metaphysics,* about religion; *Poetics,* about literature; and *Politics,* about **government.**

Interested in everything

Aristotle was interested in everything. He made lists of the winners of the **Olympic Games**, the best plays, and the forms of government in Greek cities. He wrote about "**barbarian** customs," and put together an **encyclopedia** of natural history.

He tried to answer questions based on what he saw. This was an important lesson for future scientists.

◀ **This Roman statue shows Aristotle thinking. Of his hundreds of books, only 47 are known today.**

How Aristotle's ideas survived

After Aristotle's death, the Lyceum continued. One story tells how Aristotle's books passed to a friend, and ended up in a moldy cellar. In about 60 B.C.E., Andronicus of Rhodes, the last head of the Lyceum, rescued the books and published them.

The Romans admired Aristotle greatly, but from 500–1100 C.E., he was almost forgotten in Europe. Then, in 1204, **crusaders** from Europe captured the city of Constantinople (modern Istanbul, Turkey), and brought home copies of Aristotle's works. In this way, Aristotle was rediscovered by the West.

For a long time, Aristotle's ideas were the basis for all science. His ideas on drama were held up as rules for writing plays. Today, Aristotle is no longer so important, but his ideas are at the core of the way people in the West think, and of many of the things they do.

▲ Aristotle's ideas were studied in the Arab world. This picture from a Turkish manuscript, from the thirteenth century C.E., shows Aristotle (right) teaching science to students.

Glossary

archaeologist person who finds out about the past by studying the remains of buildings and other objects

barbarian to the Greeks, anyone who spoke a foreign language

biology scientific study of living things

bronze metal made by mixing melted copper and tin

bust statue of a person's head and shoulders

charcoal special already-burned wood, used as fuel

citizen member of a state or nation

civilization highly developed, organized society

colony settlement founded by a country in another place

conqueror ruler who seizes other lands or peoples by force

court physician doctor who works for a ruler in the ruler's palace

crusader European soldier who fought in the Holy Land (Palestine) during the Middle Ages

democracy "rule by the people;" a political system in which everyone has a say in the government

discus saucer-shaped object, thrown by an athlete

empire large land or group of lands ruled by one person or government

encyclopedia book or books containing information about one or many subjects

exile being forced to leave one's home to live elsewhere

government system under which a place or people is ruled

historian person who studies and writes about the past

javelin type of spear thrown by a soldier or athlete

loincloth piece of cloth worn hanging down from the waist in front and back

naturalist person who studies animals and plants

Olympic Games in ancient Greece, a festival of sports held to honor the gods

oracle sacred place where Greeks went to consult a god or goddess about their future

papyrus reed used to make paper, or the kind of paper made from reeds; invented in Egypt

Persia country in Asia (modern Iran)

philosopher thinker who tries to understand the world, the purpose of the universe, and the nature of human life; Greek for "someone who loves knowledge"

politician person involved in government matters

politics business of government

revolt uprising by people against their rulers

scroll ancient book made from a long roll of papyrus or animal skin (parchment), wrapped around two wooden sticks

slave servant who is the property of his or her master or mistress

soul part of a person that many people believe causes us to think or behave as we do. In some religions, the soul is believed to live on after the body dies.

tomb burial place, often marked by a stone or a building

treason crime of plotting against a ruler or government

treaty formal agreement made between countries

tunic loose garment, often sleeveless, that reaches just above the knees

tutor teacher hired to teach a child at home

university place where many subjects are taught at an advanced level

Time Line

399 B.C.E.	Death of the **philosopher** Socrates
384 B.C.E.	Aristotle is born in Stagira, in northeastern Greece
367 B.C.E.	Aristotle travels to Athens to study with Plato
347 B.C.E.	Plato dies
344 B.C.E.	Aristotle studies nature on the island of Lesbos
338 B.C.E.	Philip of Macedonia rules all Greece
336 B.C.E.	Philip dies, and his son Alexander becomes king of Greece
335 B.C.E.	Aristotle founds the Lyceum school in Athens
323 B.C.E.	Death of Alexander the Great
322 B.C.E.	Aristotle dies
750 C.E.	Arabs spread the religion of Islam, and preserve the writings of Aristotle in the East
1200s C.E.	**Crusaders** bring Aristotle's ideas from the East to western Europe

Pronunciation Guide

Word	You say
Achilles	a-KILL-eez
Aegean	ih-JEE-an
agora	AG-er-ah
Chaeronea	CARE-uh-NEE-ah
Chalcis	KAL-sis
chiton	KIGH-ten
Euboea	You-BEE-ah
Hippocrates	Hip-PAH-kra-teez
Knossos	NOSS-us
Lyceum	lie-SEE-um
Pericles	PARE-ih-kleez
phalanx	FAY-lanks
Pythias	PITH-ee-us
Sappho	SAFF-o
Stagira	Sta-JYE-rah

More Books to Read

Kerr, Daisy. *Ancient Greeks*. Danbury, Conn.: Franklin Watts, 1997.

Rees, Rosemary. *The Ancient Greeks*. Chicago: Heinemann Library, 1997. An older reader can help you with this book.

Taylor, Pat. *The Ancient Greeks*. Chicago: Heinemann Library, 1997.

Index